AMNESIA

Jonah Winter

T0345755

Amnesia

Jonah Winter

Oberlin College Press

www.oberlin.edu/ocpress

Grateful acknowledgment is made to the following journals, which first published some of the poems in this volume: *Chicago Review, Exquisite Corpse, FIELD, Hawaii Review, Ironwood, New Voices: The Academy of American Poets University and College Prize Anthology 1984-1988, The St. Mark's Poetry Project Newsletter, and ZING!*

Publication of this book was supported in part by a grant from the Ohio Arts Council.

Ohio Arts Council
A STATE AGENCY
THAT SUPPORTS PUBLIC
PROGRAMS IN THE ARTS

Library of Congress Cataloging-in-Publication Data

Winter, Jonah.
  Amnesia / Jonah Winter.
  (The FIELD Poetry Series v. 16)
  I. Title.   II. Series.

LC: 2004101363
ISBN: 0-932440-96-7   (pbk.)

For Eberle

Contents

I

Psalm

Emptying the trash,
going to sleep at night,
just daring to speak
in any language to anyone:

Our prayers are answered,
even if the words we say
                    are just dreamt-of
admissions of love to strangers,
unsent letters
shoved away, forgotten, at dawn,
like street lights turned off
as the sky begins to gray
                    above the black fields—
all of this is being written down somewhere.

See. Even that ladder leaning up against the barn
wants to make you feel better.
See how easily the dew collects on its white slats,
the way the morning hardly breathes?

See that man who drinks himself to sleep,
how his face is pressed against the kitchen table—
see how the light from his kitchen shines through the window
    of the old farmhouse?
Somebody sees that light.

The Garden of Crows

This is how the leaves unfold at dawn:

a prayer
for nothing's ears
far away,

an ochre field
recovering
its black dream.

★★★

I am small.
I am a small word
like and or the.

I am any
patch of grass
in the garden of crows.

I am barely audible, like a train
you hear at night,

like an attic you won't go into much,

like a gate to someone else's house,

like a town on a map, whose name you say.

Variation on a Theme by Copernicus

Somewhere in the woods, an acorn falls.

It is the center of the world.

So is the odd rock
        no one's seen yet.

And someone clambering down
the steep path finds himself

to be like a voice
breaking the silence of cedars,

speaking to no one
and everything
all at once:

the everything spoken to
seems to listen
closely, and without a word

for miles,
all the way out to the end
of a broken pier

in nowhere, which is pink.

Ex Nihilo

A face appears in the window.

Hours later, a face appears in the window.

Some years are like that.

You might be zipping up a windbreaker.
The sky might be an old photograph.
You might be in that photograph,

just the back of your head,
                        your collar turned up.

When you light the match,
it goes out so quick

you might not see the flame.

Missing Panels from an Altarpiece

The man behind the glass at the all-night filling station counting out bills.

The hills of old snow on the roadside, growing older.

Occasional headlights
from nowhere, flaring up, then:

★

Slag heaps, salt piles, a long row of telephone poles
over miles of crystalline farmland:
sparkling, an agnus dei turned into weather,
with no one on the radio to mind much.

★

My mother once said
you do what you do
                    and let other people put a label on it.
Just then my grandfather stepped into the room
holding up a needlepoint rendition
of Leonardo's "Last Supper."
He had used blue thread for the saints' faces,
and Jesus Christ was orange.

The image is a toll-booth, and I
am searching through my pocket for some change.

The Ecstasy According to St. Lucy

The Hallelujah chorus
sung by a choir of deaf-mutes
lost in the wilderness
late in December, the muted dusk

filtering through panels of stained glass
left in the ruined cathedral
the snow blows in
for several midnights:

the voice that cryeth
cryeth for no ears,
the hand that reacheth
grasps at empty air:

a pact between nothing and nothing
signed with invisible ink,
delivered by four blind horsemen
trampling a path through the forest of dreams

where lives the old witch, tending her fire
hours and hours,
just this pot of coffee
by which to stay awake:

I have traveled far
as the night extends, rich
in its estuaries
packed with sleeping fish—

and all I have brought back
is this:
Branched, dove-lit,
Magenta, ossified, fossilized,

Malachite and conglomerate, hidden,
Up-turned, sometimes, dried,
Burnt sienna and hard to believe,
Acorn Paradise, brown-barked:

Now's burial ground, Memory's hair
Braided there in the grave,
Dogrun solstice, leafage
Small, enclosed, searched through and raked

Between stepping stones, statues
To exhaustion… China, far away,
The miniature spade, hacked roots, hoed
Dirt, the promised hole.

Mojo

Killing the spider,
I create

an object, a new
space,

a shrine of exits,
a hiding place

I can't know
in this life,

blind as a vine
obscured in the jungle,

a blue spot
on a black wing.

Still Lives

Horn of the stuffed rhinoceros,
dull sheen of his hide, marble shine
of his eyes, black hole
back of his stiff lips.

Sea lions, killer whales
half above the solid water. Tortoises
almost on the bank, plasticine
palm trees, painted mountains, perpetual

nightfall over Minnesota, blue snow
falling from morning to evening, always
the same dim light, always the gray wolf
leaping toward the glass which divides us.

Stranger

You are the entire year
of 1962,
with its dark glasses
and swimming pools at night,
its live oaks,
its fishing nets,
its afternoons.
It's raining.
There are no street signs.
There is, however,
a Chinese restaurant
a block away,
and you're inside it
sipping tea.
I can barely see you
through the rain
and the golden letters.
My lips are moving
and I might be
saying something.

Sleep

How under the pier
the water gets darker.

How inside the box, the nails
touch each other.

How an orange
rolls away from the other oranges.

How the pillow
fits your head by morning.

Hallelujah!

Just when you thought the world was a crossword puzzle
scribbled in some celestial newspaper, day after day
a different solution—God descends from the heavens
playing an accordion

II

Postcards from Paradise

Lake Somnambulist,
Choir of Tears,

black dahlia
the shape of a galaxy,

window lake,
hackberry murk

montaged on mannequins' legs,
rain

in the telephone wires,
statues of Jesus,

palm fronds
poised in the shadow pool,

three-piece suit,
calm of linoleum,

trees wearing nothing, black
and resounding with talk.

*

I remember being alone
like an ocean, each day
a wave, greenish-gray,
each night black with fish
and flotsam
              from other people's lives.

★★★

Sunday umbrella,
D-Train from the Bronx,

arduous sand of the found shell
coating a pocket,

the furnished apartment
above a liquor store,

the stranger at the window
disappearing inside

the rest of his life,
nails sticking up

from the boardwalk,
a century of parasols

thinning out
on the long beach, dogs

rummaging September,
the trash heaps:

fish bones,
dolls' heads,

columns of news,
various mollusks.

★

At the Hotel of Stars
I rang and I rang
the night bell: No one came
to the desk.
Mirrors emptied themselves into corridors,
carpets flushed with memory
into the night of what was
                              a ballroom.

★★★

Pillars of the Clouds,
dry leaf

marking the next page
of history:

just as before,
there's the priest

at the gates
of the black cathedral

surrounded by skyscrapers
and derelicts,

plastic azaleas
on tombstones,

there's the tall man
with the black umbrella

and wing-tip shoes,
just as before

it's five o'clock,
it's raining,

there's someone to meet,
it's already dark.

★

The cheesecake at Café Death
was marvelous. I asked
for a napkin, they gave me
a deck of cards,
a miniature fountain. I asked
for the bill, they brought me
a green angel,
a year of snow.

★★★

In an Arctic breath,
an iceberg

floats past an arm
recognizably alive.

The angel descends,
speaking gibberish,

carrying a scroll
without words.

What was a picture
of a violin

is a cloud
full of old clothes.

Where there were people,
now there are statues.

★

You will know me
by my white wings:
heavy as things, they drag,
drag the checkered tiles
in the Palace of Jars:
everything is preserved
as if yesterday were today,
as if I were alive.

★★★

Alarm clocks ring
in the Valley of Clouds.

No one gets up.
In the Hotel of Stars

there are many vacancies
at dawn,

acorns and maple leaves
falling, falling

past the black dog
and the factory,

past the cathedral,
past its ruins,

past the night watchman
asleep in his guard booth.

You are sleeping too
outside your house.

It's drizzling.
Your reading lamp is on.

★

You are old as the storm.
You are old as October.
Fish in the harbor of sleep
swim through your name.
You are the North Star.
You are the boulder
no one has seen,
an icon nailed to a plaster wall.
Your birth is a garden
black as the apocalypse.

★★★

Greetings
from the constellation

Obscurity:
Draw your own lines

from oranges
to crucifix,

from candle burning
to rain,

from gilded frame
in the Museum of Lips

to catfish
flapping on the boardwalk:

try to connect
trenchcoat to opera,

subway tunnel
to blue eyes,

mint leaves
to graffiti...

★

The weather here is Sunday
all week long: the rain
rains from the same place,
white as a house—palm trees
thrashing frond against frond, and umbrellas
inverting, gesturing to the wind
to make it stop.

★★★

Albino dog,
chestnut husks,

sidewalks, Christ,
his entry through

exit doors, stars,
the February horse,

motionless, its hoofs,
its black blinders,

the coffin,
your corpse ripening

like a clock
without hands.

★

I had wanted to give you a place
where you could walk, a park
where you could watch seasons change,
the path beneath the elms
snow-covered, haunted with squirrels,
rows of benches, empty,
and you with a long scarf, walking away
towards the forsythia,
the entrance to spring a stone arch
still wet from Tuesday's rain,
last year's leaves still plastered to the mud,
black rock embankments pocked with old snow
so you would have loved
                    thinking of me.

III

Descent from the Ceiling of Heaven

When, at last, Michaelangelo
climbs down the scaffold
from the ceiling of heaven:

farther away,
farther away than carrion crows
in the Caucasus Mountains,

farther away than the goat
whose blue eyes
mirror my tomorrow:

a sky so blue
it isn't the sky—however specked
with classical figures floating

stone-like through the air
in a waltz
choreographed

by the faceless director
of iron grates and drain pipes
under the streets and the park...   All

as beautiful as snow
falling through the night
on the city,

the wrong Magnificat
played on the organ
by someone hidden, blithe

as plastic grapes
hanging from the trellis
in the Torch Café,

the body of a saint
stinking so badly, pale,
laid out

in some rented room
darker than the dark sleep
of shoes:

and here's the candle,
and here's the forest,
and here—connect them, place one

inside the other, tonight,
when you stand, raw as a wolf
in the piazza,

howling to the unresponsive moon
for sympathy
or meaning:

some background noise disturbs you,
an ice-cream cart wheels past,
pedaled by the shadow of a man

who has dropped a package
wrapped in brown paper
and bound with a thick string

that you will spend your days
and nights untying.

Exodus

"The tree may not be escaped from by means of the tree."

—Francis Ponge

The world is full of sanctuaries:
restrooms, museums, thighs
interlocking with thighs

late winter afternoons,
the elevator cage
springing open

to the mournful hymns
of the fourteenth century:
I am the black umbrella

of solitude, flowering
shoelace,
unpainted canvas

of now, the puddle
altered by anything, rain,
a leaf, footfalls, a face

for an instant
then clouds or crows
unravel the long braid

of chance:
crickets and lightning
sing their duet

with a wind ostinato,
the portrait speaks
to the table

that isn't listening
or pretends to be something else,
a rug,

a wet match sizzling
on Fourteenth Street,
telling its story

to a storefront reflection
full of actions
yet absolutely still, attentive

as a child examining a rock
or a finger that's bleeding,
escaping itself through itself:

the lighthouse
continues its drawn-out search,
a desk lamp

illumines a woman's hands
sewing something
back together,

the hours
condensing like knives
in a silverware drawer

that closes over and over
in time to a scratchy recording
of Jimmie Rodgers

singing T
for Texas, T
for Tennessee—I am lonely

for a past
that's not mine, a southhood
stilted, stiff as Aunt Alamo

standing her ground
behind the lazy-boy chair
where Aunt Alga sits

Bible-silent,
her eyes two vigilant
votive candles fixed

on me, who just
floats away in a sailor suit
towards nineteenth-century France:

Good-bye—
It was wonderful
really, I

thought the plaster squid
that hung from the ceiling of Garguillo's
was real,

real as anything
in the world
that could be said

while champagne bottles
pop and spew
on the balcony

where I make this toast
to you
out there on the sand

fronting the evening tide
and clanging
buoy—happy

to just be
who I am,
wearing a black suit

during my procession
away from everything,
balloons, knife-throwers,

voices in bars
that fuse into one voice
saying

good-bye, I say
walking backwards
again down the wide sidewalk

away from the museum
in the thunder shower,
umbrellaless...

Entrances to the World

Everything, a front porch, snow,
Mozart, exhaust fumes
curling from tailpipes in the cold

and shoreboatless days,
tall weeds you break off in the vacant lot
late in the year, the fires

burning like mirrors
hiding their pasts with impeccable nows—
into which you sink your hands

and dive headlong through your reflection
into the city where all things go backwards,
the clocks, the men who carry ladders,

the moon, your own steps
back to the bookstores,
back to your apartment, night after night,

all in slow motion,
an untranslatable quiet, like oceans
inside the ears of the deaf, inside a leaf

the conversations you would hear
if you were God:
everything speaks—

if you were only patient
as air, you would hear
the endless telegraph of footsteps

on a sidewalk, you would hear
the small sounds that fill a house—
the creaking wood, the long pauses, doors

and the resolute clicks of doorknobs—
as sentences drawn out
over hours and hours,

years, a poem
imageless, opaque
as the ice-block

relieved from the rope that lowered it
onto the loading dock
in the hot East Texas town

where my father was born
and lived in a small white house
by the Cady railroad, until

he was seventeen,
and like the mongrel they'd chained to the hackberry tree
forever, escaped

to the rain
and the small white house
where I was born, and lived, until

my grandfather stood at the screen door,
turned towards the field he'd brought
from Illinois: before long, I wake,

falling through the open night
of my grave: it's a Greyhound station
and Pompeii's bleary-eyed immortals stay up

in the plastic chairs
of a waiting room
embalmed in the blizzard

that only snows when I shake it:
the glass dome is glued
to the base of the world

where the village is:
angels take turns trumpeting
over the candles

house after house
on Christmas Eve,
smorgasbords and steins laid out

for no one…
The stove is turned on low,
the borscht

steams the windows
of the loft,
black bread

warms in the oven, and I
am glad to be inside
chopping garlic, drinking wine

with you
who've come to visit me
in the almost dark.

Where are you?
I've set out a bowl and spoon
at the table, and

don't tell me you're not here.
Are you
hiding in a book, are you

a lake,
are you mad at me
because I'm here and you're

the blade of an axe
as it withdraws, or
are you the stone pietà

alone in the sky
with the Pleiades
crying like a symphony?

Do you sleep, ever?
Would you like
an ashtray

or a little piece of metal,
a postcard,
a ticket stub?

Revelations

After the Year of Mirrors
and after the cadenzas,
after the century plant

blooms like a death wish, at dawn,
the red sky arched like a cape
of the matador who stands

upright behind the seen world,
after the thresholds of ecstasy
open and then close:

black train, that infinity
always off in the background,
a straight line leading nowhere

which is a town that looks like
the town you grew up in, still
as a barber shop, Sunday

afternoon, red brick façade
vanishing the moment you touch it —
after that, then what?

IV

Amnesia

You are my statue, my little Renaissance,
you are an onyx, a shoreline, upon your black rocks
I fling my twenty autumns. Red leaves fall.
Caught up in the sky's thoughts, I cry like a door.

I like how unattainable you are:
Beatrice, dusk, the grand illusion:
a rush of distant traffic from the highway
sounding in the inch between our lips—

our lips, now absent, touching like a fugue
touching the stained glass and the Blessed Face.
Only now do I realize the past
contains us perfectly: how still we are

there, by the celadon waves, in the North,
containing, together, two distinct horizons.
The snow, the snow, the fire, the snow, the snow.

The snow, the snow, the fire, the snow, the snow.
The eucalyptus tree, arbitrarily.
Then, like a week of rain, the grizzly bear
chanting your hymn: your skin is a cold wind…

I sleep occasionally. Meanwhile, seals bark
on the black rocks. What are you thinking now?
O you whose veil is the night sky in the west.
(O ridiculous fan, stirring the meaningless air!)

Nothing I say ever points to anything
larger—for instance, the ocean.
The point is not to name, the point
is to rename, to speak to the plastic rose

as if you, Beatrice, were inside it,
completely present—I float through your tresses.
I enter your eyes through which the clouds pass.

I enter your eyes through which the clouds pass.
I unbutton your blouse. It's spring. Tchaikovsky's
Violin Concerto in D Major
won't get out of my head. O, it's spring!

It's winter: still dark. The road to the station
darkened even more by snow-covered spruce,
the iron foundry blue and laid to rest
beneath the weight of the long night. Where are you?

Everywhere? Tuesday? Paradise? How
do you climb down from the stars without a ladder?
How do you survive between the lips
and the junkyard, the moon and everything else?

The harvest moon, the date-palms and the boat
that takes me there, the rocking, the silent fish
in silent chambers, some small sound like a word.

In silent chambers, some small sound like a word
wakes you, Beatrice, but you do not move.
The medieval tapestries cloister your future.
Go back to sleep. Now the leaves are falling.

Your bedroom is the ocean. You are the waves.
The flocks of cormorants that troubled your dreams
have changed into seagulls. The earth is flat!
Look, there's Zeus in the west with his cheeks puffed out!

There's a brontosaurus and some palm trees.
Oh no, day and night are being invented.
What state am I in? Mr. Brakeman, uh:
"I haven't got a nickel, not a penny…"

Eurydice, what brings you here? Why don't you look at me
now as we walk between the broken columns?
I get this feeling that I'm not alive.

I get this feeling that I'm not alive.
I lie between two cypresses at night
with open eyes. Nothing moves. A bead
of water containing the moon hangs from a leaf.

You. You in a white gown, for a second
you're nearer. Something changes. A silver jug
pours the rest of the flat crimson sky
into my ear and you're gone. Now there's a mountain.

And sometimes you speak in a far-off voice
softer than bed-sheets. And mangoes fall
all the night. And sometimes the ice plant
chants like a choir behind a convent wall.

These days, when the dog-star is afraid
of how the waves might react, or the pier,
I am sure, my love, I might be a statue.

I am sure, my love, I might be a statue.
In fact, moonflowers toss in the wind
and drop from your hair to my stone lips and then
scatter to the pavement and pause like dawn.

(You are only a surface, a lake, containing
chaos beneath you, factories, somnambulists
like you, who stand so still against the wall
in a posture of crucifixion, you Expressionist:

Not where I am! aslant in the slanting city,
alive again among the burning candles
and icons and oceans and tree of the black leaf
and masks confronting death in every reflection—)

Something is dreadfully wrong for I feel…undone
about the way the eucalyptus looks
like you with a torch in an underwater age.

Like you with a torch in an underwater age,
like nothing, like everything that can't be said,
like Villa-Lobos en la Cantina Espejo,
like "here are the lights along the Jersey shore,"

like your hand, like even thinking at all
about impossibility—marble steps
I climb toward the checkerboard table
of all days and all nights, marsala

wine in a glass encompassed by your sky
because you breathe, and because the salmon galaxies
offer their leaves of catalpa, drooping down
one from every star, and you own them all

because you breathe, and nothing hurts, and today
I hoist myself into the jaws of Leviathan.
Will the shell become the ocean again?

Will the shell become the ocean again?
Will the subway token of noon
drop into its metal slot, much longer?
Here is a week of rain and a breath:

Hold on to them. Don't let anyone touch them.
And here are some leaves, but you cannot see them.
And I cannot see you. Air is air
and I cannot replace it with leaves or you.

Here is the rest of my life, a makeshift boat
for you: Travel as far away as you can.
One thing I must tell you now—the outboard-motor
doesn't work. Ditch it. Use an oar.

I have learned to dance. Follow me out to the pasture.
But you cannot walk through this pasture, I think:
Air is air, and I cannot replace it with leaves.

Air is air, and I cannot replace it with leaves.
Francesca, will the night of the night of the night...
Could you press your lithe fingers against mine,
could you pass the Northern Lights, please...

Snowing, snowing. This long wooden table,
this kerosene lamp and this black bread.
Our faces, in chiaroscuro, hollowing out
a space in the darkness. Pour me some Benedictine.

O the world inside the pine inside
the branch inside the owl inside
you inside. (Look how many months
hide in the eaves, furtive, unconvinced.)

What is this dark and tawny music? Is it
Sibelius's birthday? Is it January
already, is it night? Are we there yet?

Is it night? Are we there yet? I think it's possible
to say alacanthus bloom and mean something
different: lighthouse or indefinite morning.
I think I would like to rename the world:

you. O marble steps, I think I will call you
Atlantic Ocean—tomorrow
I will set sail in my cerulean boat
towards the great bronze doors

of St. Peter's Cathedral.
Everything belongs to me, and nothing does.
About the ceiling of the universe, I'll just say
all of us are up there, town after town,

the closed shops, the rain, and many nights
in the peach-blossom skin of the cherubs…

V

The Black Hole

In the beginning,
there was not much of anything,

a few palm trees, weather,
one dinosaur

off in the painted background
where everything began

and continues to begin
as someone paints over

the yucca plant, contained now, immortal,
replaced by a telephone booth

where I've been for the past two years
(it's raining, primordially)

trying your number—
oh but it's been disconnected

just as the German Shepherd's howl,
disembodied in the infinite forest,

suggests a growing distance
only the leaves answer..

★

In the beginning, the rosewood casket of dawn
unlocks, and what's inside

looks like a Texas landscape:
a long unvarying horizon, a few mesquite trees and a truck

that takes someone from Point A to Point B in the lifting dark
eschatologically, barbeque stands

and filling stations vanishing always
in the Blue Northern and the rearview mirror

the highway enters, cloistered
in its own diminishing infinity, lacking exit

or audience—nothing moves or breathes
on the other side of the mirror:

it's a swamp filled with statues
of everyone who ever looked at themselves, quieted then

and now, the seer and the seen, like binary stars,
always changing places…

★

In the beginning,
you will not understand

everything, what it means
that anything can happen

once the eyelids are shut
and the banners stop flapping,

the boxcars, the orange sky,
long lines of immigrants

in photographs, fragments
of long-coats, months,

you, in a sense,
being a door.

Resistance

The expressionless teller at the First Virginia Bank or
the black fabric of your stockings or
the darkness of a closed news stand or
the way it feels to lie face down on Nineteenth Street.

The way the night shovels away the day,
the way two walls push each other back,
the way the airport bar empties out
and the leather bar-stools look like serious drinkers.

And you went home and cried for three months.
And I brought you an apple wrapped in paper.
And I sat for hours in your kitchen chair
which, with help from the bright fluorescent lights,

kept me from falling through to the cellar
of Valhalla, as when we're lying by each other
and each of our bodies is keeping us both
apart.

Event Horizon in Bar Valhalla, New York

It rains I'm in England.
It's almost tea-time. Suddenly I love to read
and overcook vegetables.

Months pass—it snows
I'm in Russia. It seems that I've
lost all my reindeer. They wandered into the night...

They'll come back someday, I think, cheered on
by the sight of a diner I'm in Montana
now in some kind of relation with the pending sky...

And it's endless—your face, for instance,
reminds me of the Dallas Public Library
when it's closed.

Don't be offended: I like it best
then, when it's closed, those dark windows
and potted plants, all those words

by themselves, performing, captive,
trees falling down in books,
stars falling down, Venus on a half-shell, rising...

But like I was saying (Could I have another one?)
all things are revelations
of betrayal: a cigarette machine

becomes a sunrise in El Paso
as you unhinge yourself
from room to room, year to year,

nail to nail, walls change to scenes
of Pompeii, of ruins
unstopped each moment in the deep blue—

so that the orange extinguish of daylight
is a prayer in a rain–lit cathedral
that plays on a tape recorder which

I just happen to have
if you've got a moment, while I
unload this bag of statues—

The "Unexpected Mariachi Band" Factor

or

Logic 101

or

Why Poets Weren't Allowed in Plato's Republic

or

The Nature of Things

or

Would You Buy a Used Car from This Poem?

or

Poetry

or

Hi I'm a Philosophy Major

The wind, like a retired fisherman
checking his mailbox in the morning,
but finding nothing there, in the tropical half-light of pre-rain,
subsequently retreating into unlit quarters
never to be seen again,

stops. And so it goes:
A woman takes a bath.
A man paints a picture of her without any clothes.
Years later, we see her in the Met:
She's still bending over.

All of this is like a blue horse
which is somehow also the night sky
filled with stars.
It gallops across the field behind our eyes
and travels far.

X = Y.
Y becomes disconsolate.
X, through osmosis, starts to cry.
After much deliberation, both depart
on a breezy, moonlit voyage to Z.

The Singularity

Some sort of archangelical hero sandwich
(slash) vacuum-cleaner which, miraculously,
contains things
larger than itself—Paris, for instance,

la rue du Poisson Noir
at dawn, when the shades are drawn
still, when the mirrors in haberdasheries
perform their tableaux vivants, the mannequins

and cash registers signifying nothing
which leads me to an overwhelming question:
if I cried out tonight, in some imaginary woods,
who, out there, among the frozen children,

the statues in the old witch's garden,
would come back to life?
Or would my voice be like a snow
falling on their little marble hands

while the charred body in the oven
remembered itself into existence again
by inhabiting everything, including
your eyelids, which are getting very heavy—

You want to go to sleep...sleep...but
beware of the icicles' thickening
on the eaves of certain Lithuanian houses.
Nothing can touch you there, and yet

you pause in the doorway, still holding on
to the brass doorknob.
Nothing can hear you there, and yet
already the sound of sleigh-bells wakes you.

Hotel of the Stars

Alain and Elaine go to the Hotel of the Stars. There, they see a huge room with many lights. Where are the fathers? Do you hear the voices? Or—is it raining?

★

Where is the train station? Excuse me, sir, but the night arrives quickly. And, it is necessary that we arrive at the forest before the moon is full. The time: eight fifty-eight, eight fifty-nine, eight fifty-nine and a half...

★

Nine o'clock. The drinks are blue. Thank you for the shadows. It is very very delicious. It is a woman on the table. Why is she crying? Where is the symphony? Where is the *the*?

★

What time is it? The baggage comes. Thank you for the directions. I love you a million times. I love you for a million years. It is necessary that I laugh. Perhaps, you see me? Yes? Here is the baggage.

★

Repeat: Alain and Elaine are very tired. Alain and Elaine are very tired. Very good. Now, repeat: Alain and Elaine do not know how to close their eyes. Alain and Elaine do not know how to close their eyes. Good. Now: a, b, c, d...

★

Alain and Elaine decide to enter the mirror. Very good. Good-bye, Alain and Elaine. It is not too bad. We have many flowers. Would you like a rose? Where is the money? What is the money?

★

What is the fish? The fish is a blue fish. Thank you. Thank you. How do we arrive at the door? You arrive at the door. Thank you. You arrive at the door by crossing the park. Thank you. You do not arrive at the door. Thank you.

About the Author

Jonah Winter is the author and illustrator of several children's books, including *Diego* (Knopf, 1992), *Frida* (Scholastic, 2002), and *BEISBOL! Latino Baseball Pioneers and Legends* (Lee & Low, 2001). His poems have appeared in many journals, including *Field, The Antioch Review, The Threepenny Review, Chicago Review,* and *Ploughshares.* His poem "Sestina: Bob," which first appeared in *Ploughshares,* was chosen for the *Pushcart Anthology 2001.* His first book of poems, *Maine,* was selected in 2002 by David Lehman for Slope Editions as its inaugural book prize winner.